When Piggy was a Swine

AF587439

When Piggy was a Swine

Guava Press, Blue Tang Ltd., Newmarket, ON L3X 2R6, Canada
ISBN 978-1-927395-97-4
Printed in India

Adapted from a traditional Jamaican rhyme

Written by **Al Campbell**

Illustrated by **Sanjana Singh**

OINK!

Once upon a time
when Piggy was a swine,

She jumped over a clothesline
and hurt her behind.

“Hurry, hurry!” said Piggy the swine.
“Please send for Doctor Valentine.”

OINK

The good doctor
was just in time
with a pint
of turpentine

And a bottle
of plain white lime,
to rub on poor little
Piggy's sore behind.

One Monday before Christmastime,
Piggy ate Farmer John's potato vine.

Farmer John thought it was a big crime,
so he took bold action and didn't whine.

He grabbed Piggy by her fat waistline,
and tied her legs tightly with long twine.

Off he ran to the high court that daytime,
and carried on his back the squealing swine.

The judge heard the case before lunchtime. He said, “I don’t think a pig can do a crime!”

So that was the first and last known time a pig was charged for eating a potato vine.

There was also another sad and interesting time, when poor Piggy ate a bucket of green limes.

The limes tasted worse than salty brine,
and a gulp of water didn't help the swine.

Piggy ran all the way to the coastline,
and jumped into the sea to drink it like wine.

The silly pig was only saved by the divine,
because there was a floating grapevine

That got wrapped around her fat waistline,
and a boy pulled her back to the coastline.

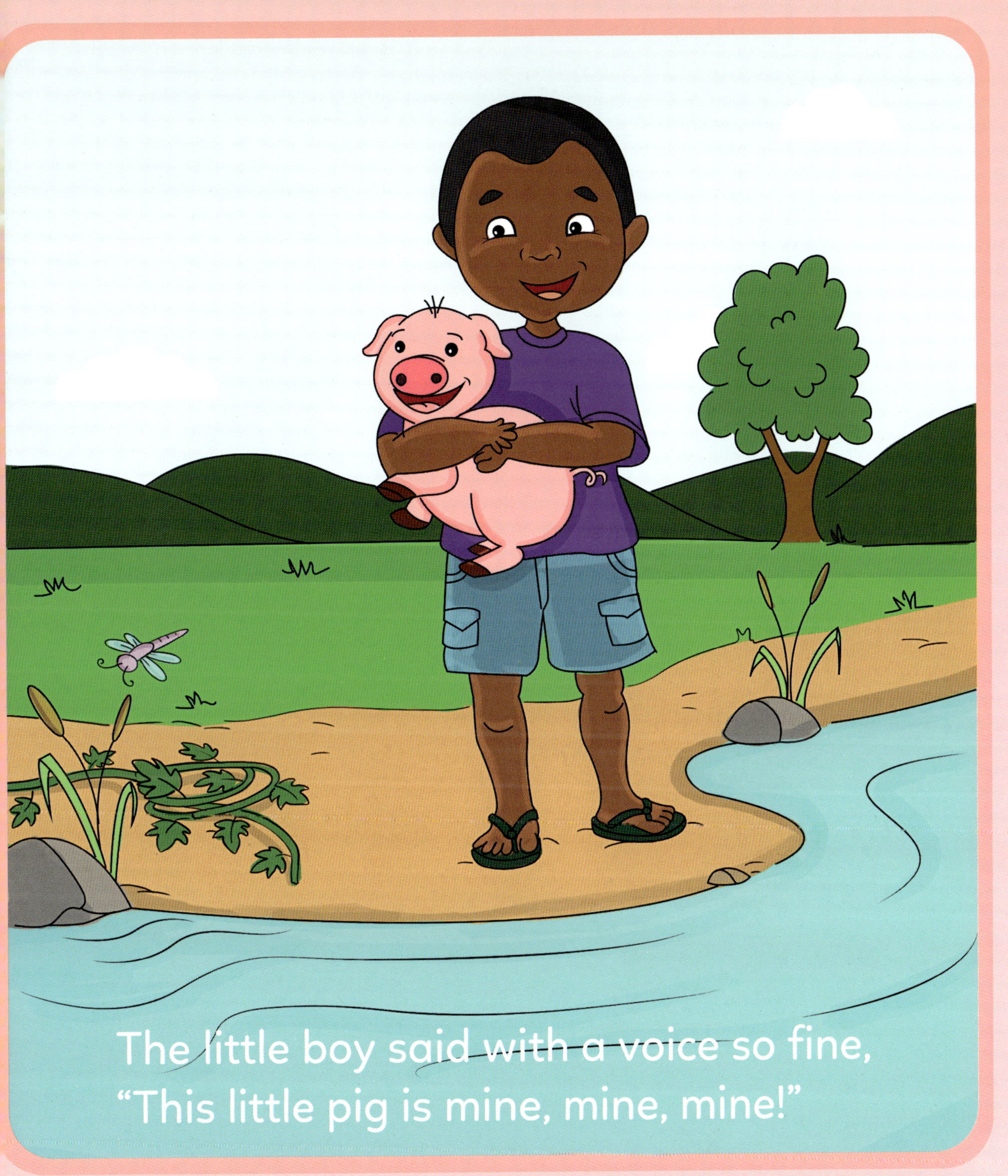

The little boy said with a voice so fine,
"This little pig is mine, mine, mine!"

Piggy lived to see many days of sunshine,

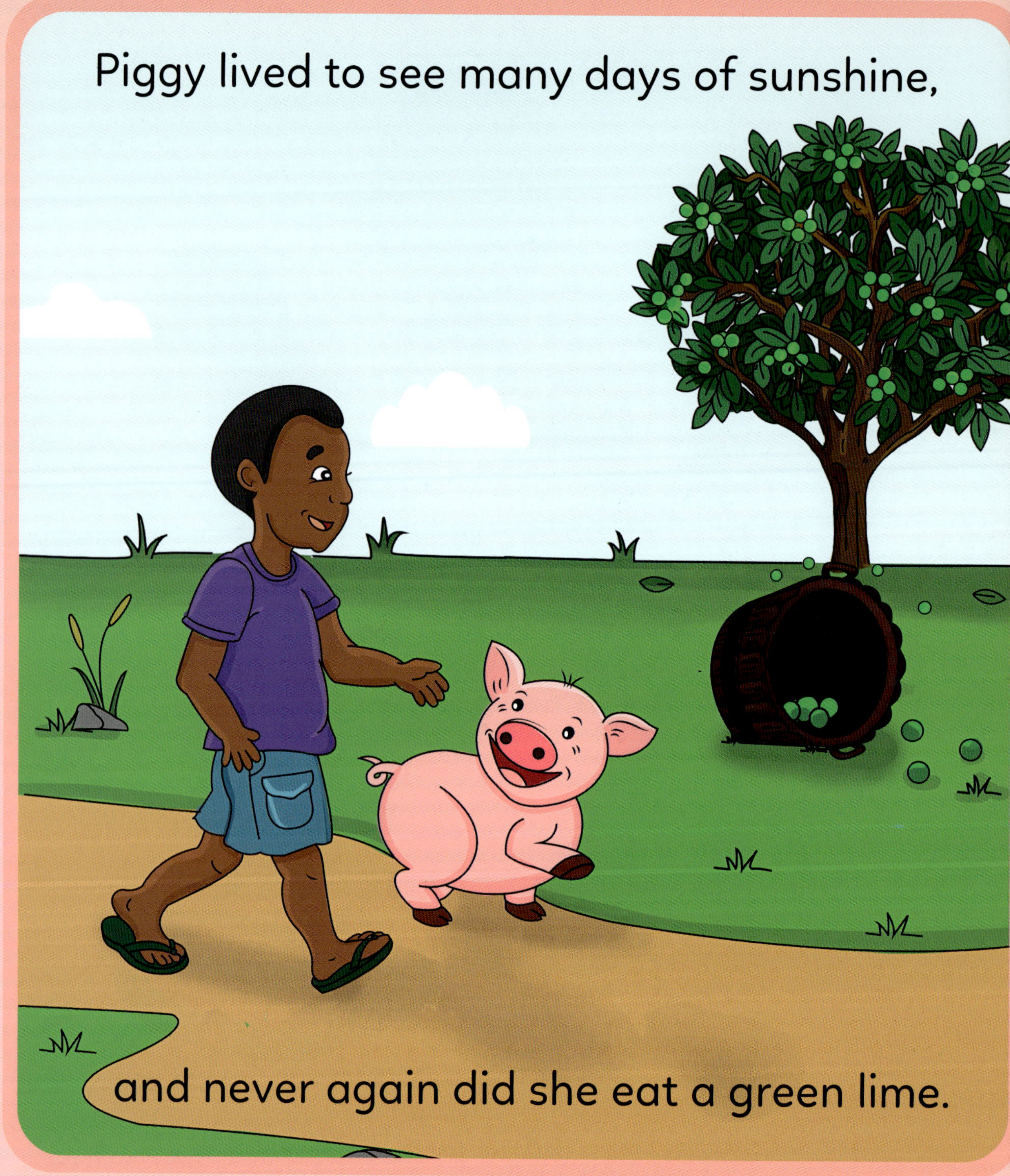

and never again did she eat a green lime.

Piggy also stays far from any potato vine,
and never again jumped over a clothesline.

Today Piggy is
not a mere swine.
Piggy's loved by all
and lives on cloud nine.

Pig Songs and Proverbs

This Little Piggy

This little piggy went to market.
This little piggy stayed home.
This little piggy had roast meat.
This little piggy had none.
And this little piggy went
"Wee, Wee, Wee," all the way home!

To Market, To Market

To market, to market, to buy a fat pig,
Home again, home again, jiggety-jig.

To market, to market, to buy a fat hog,
Home again, home again, jiggety-jog.

To market, to market to buy a fruit cake,
Home again, home again, market is late.

To market, to market, to buy a fruit bun,
Home again, home again, market is done.

Pigs in the Mud

Roll, roll, roll around
In the mud all day.
That is what pigs do.
What a way to play!
Roll, roll, roll around
That is how pigs play,
In a pen with a friend
On a sunny day!

The Pigs on the Farm

The pigs on the farm go,
"Oink, oink, oink,
Oink, oink, oink,
Oink, oink, oink!"

The pigs on the farm go,
"Oink, oink, oink!"
All day long.

Five Little Pigs

Five little pigs rolled in the mud
Squish, squash, squish, it sure felt good.
The farmer took a pig out,
And cleaned him up nice.

Four little pigs rolled in the mud
Squish, squash, squish, it sure felt good.
The farmer took a pig out,
And cleaned him up nice.

Three little pigs rolled in the mud
Squish, squash, squish, it sure felt good.
The farmer took a pig out,
And cleaned him up nice.

Five Little Pigs

Two little pigs rolled in the mud
Squish, squash, squish, it sure felt good.
The farmer took a pig out,
And cleaned him up nice.

One little pig rolled in the mud
Squish, squash, squish, it sure felt good.
The farmer took a pig out,
And cleaned him up nice.

No little pig rolled in the mud,
They all looked nice and clean.
The farmer turned his back
And what do you know!
All the little pigs jumped back in the mud!

Pig Proverbs

If you throw a stone into a pigsty, the pig that cries is the one you have hit.

You can't expect anything from a pig but a grunt.

Never buy a pig in a sack.

Old swines have hard snouts.

Don't cast your pearls before swines.

A little pig asked his mama why her mouth was so long, and his mama said, "Never mind, my baby, whatever made mine long will make yours long too."